Second Form Latin

Quizzes & Tests

Cheryl Lowe

MW01702654

Second Form Latin

Quizzes and Tests

by Cheryl Lowe

Published by:
Memoria Press
www.memoriapress.com

ISBN # 978-161538-085-5

 Name____________________ Date ____________

A. Vocabulary: Give dictionary form.

1. bad ____________________
2. Christ ____________________
3. debt, sin ____________________
4. earth ____________________
5. eternal ____________________
6. farmer ____________________
7. forum ____________________
8. friend ____________________
9. gift ____________________
10. girl ____________________
11. god ____________________
12. good ____________________
13. great ____________________
14. high, deep ____________________
15. horse ____________________
16. Italy ____________________
17. kingdom ____________________
18. lamb ____________________
19. lord ____________________
20. Mary ____________________
21. much ____________________
22. new ____________________
23. poet ____________________
24. queen ____________________
25. rock ____________________
26. Rome ____________________
27. sailor ____________________
28. sacred ____________________
29. sky, heaven ____________________
30. slave ____________________
31. small ____________________
32. son ____________________
33. table ____________________
34. temple ____________________
35. town ____________________
36. war ____________________
37. wide ____________________
38. word ____________________
39. world ____________________
40. year ____________________
41. one ____________________
42. two ____________________
43. three ____________________
44. four ____________________
45. five ____________________
46. six ____________________
47. seven ____________________
48. eight ____________________
49. nine ____________________
50. ten ____________________

B. Latin Sayings:

1. Roma Aeterna ______________________________
2. Anno Dómini (A.D.) ______________________________
3. ante bellum ______________________________
4. Quattuor anni témpora ______________________________
5. Mater Itáliae Roma ______________________________

C. Decline.

S.	Pl.	S.	Pl.	S.	Pl.
mensa		servus		bellum	

D. Translate.

1. fifth girl ____________________
2. sixth horse ____________________
3. four horses ____________________
4. five temples ____________________
5. ninth day ____________________

E. Translate.

1. Magnum equum videt. ______________________________

____

2. They carry many rocks. ______________________________

____

3. The small girls are praying ______________________________

____

Lesson 2 Quiz   Name____________________ Date ____________

A. Vocabulary: Give dictionary form.

1. book ________________________
2. boy, child ________________________
3. children ________________________
4. evening ________________________
5. field ________________________
6. knife ________________________
7. man ________________________
8. teacher (female) ________________________
9. teacher (male) ________________________

B. Decline.

S.	Pl.	S.	Pl.	S.	Pl.
vir		puer		ager	

C. Translate.

1. The Vatican Field ________________________
2. Liberos video. ________________________
3. Libros portas. ________________________
4. ten boys ________________________
5. We praise good men. ________________________

D. Fill in the Blanks.

1. Give the neuter rule. ________________________

____

2. What is the predicate adjective case? ________________________
3. Matins are morning prayers, and ________________________are evening prayers.
4. The ________________________belongs in the kitchen

 Name____________________ Date ____________

A. Vocabulary: Give dictionary form.

1. beautiful ______________________________
2. free ______________________________
3. lazy ______________________________
4. left, left-hand ______________________________
5. right, right-hand ______________________________
6. sacred ______________________________
7. sharp, harsh ______________________________
8. sick, ill ______________________________
9. whole, uninjured ______________________________
10. wretched ______________________________

B. Decline in singular only.

Masculine	Feminine	Neuter
integer		

C. Translate.

1. To the stars through difficulties. ______________________________.
2. sacred ground ______________________________
3. sick boy ______________________________
4. Amici amicis dona dant. ______________________________
5. The queen gave the girls gifts. ______________________________

D. Fill in the Blanks.

1. An indirect object is commonly found with verbs of ______________ or ___________.
2. In Latin the indirect object is expressed by what case? ______________________
3. An ______________________ is a whole number.

 Name____________________ Date ____________

A. Vocabulary: Give dictionary form.

1. army ____________________
2. arrival ____________________
3. bread ____________________
4. brother ____________________
5. cross ____________________
6. custom ____________________
7. day ____________________
8. dog ____________________
9. face ____________________
10. faith ____________________
11. father ____________________
12. fear ____________________
13. foot ____________________
14. fruit ____________________
15. hand ____________________
16. harbor ____________________
17. head ____________________
18. heart ____________________
19. hope ____________________
20. house ____________________
21. king ____________________
22. lake ____________________
23. lamp ____________________
24. law ____________________
25. leader ____________________
26. light ____________________
27. mother ____________________
28. name ____________________
29. peace ____________________
30. river ____________________
31. senate ____________________
32. sister ____________________
33. soldier ____________________
34. spirit ____________________
35. sun ____________________
36. thing ____________________
37. voice ____________________

B. Latin Sayings:

1. alma mater____
2. Pax Romana ____
3. Rex Regum ____
4. Carpe diem.____
5. Caput Mundi ____
6. Senatus Populusque Romanus (S.P.Q.R.)________________________

C. Decline.

Case	Singular	Plural	Singular	Plural
nom.	pater		nomen	
gen.				
dat.				
acc.				
abl.				

Case	Singular	Plural	Singular	Plural
nom.	portus		res	
gen.				
dat.				
acc.				
abl.				

D. Translate.

1. duces novi ____________________
2. spíritus liber ____________________
3. soror pulchra ____________________
4. miles ínteger ____________________
5. canes pigri ____________________
6. manus sinistra ____________________
7. pater aeger ____________________
8. wretched king ____________________
9. right foot ____________________
10. harsh laws ____________________

E. Fill in the Blanks.

1. All nouns whose genitive singular ends in ______________ are 4th declension.
2. All nouns whose genitive singular ends in ______________ are 3rd declension.
3. All nouns whose genitive singular ends in ______________ are 5th declension.
4. The ________________ singular identifies the declension of the noun and provides the stem.
5. The direct object of a verb is in the ____________________ case.

Lesson 5 Quiz Name____________________ Date ____________

A. Vocabulary: Give dictionary form.

1. bridge ____________________
2. citizen ____________________
3. city ____________________
4. enemy ____________________
5. hill ____________________
6. mountain ____________________
7. part, region ____________________
8. sea ____________________
9. ship ____________________
10. tribe ____________________

B. Decline.

Singular	Plural
pars	

Singular	Plural
mare	

C. Translate.

1. Our Sea ____________________
2. free citizens ____________________
3. the left part ____________________
4. the queen's ships ____________________
5. mother's house ____________________

D. Fill in the Blanks.

1. Third declension nouns in which the letter **i** appears in the genitive plural are called ____________________.
2. In English, possession is expressed by the preposition ____________________ or by an ____________.
3. ____________ means *in the city* and ____________ means *around the city.*
4. The UN ____________________ Plan of 1947 divided Palestine into two states.

 Name____________________ Date ____________

A. Vocabulary: Give dictionary form.

1. difficult ____________________
2. each, every, all ____________________
3. easy ____________________
4. faithful ____________________
5. heavy, serious ____________________
6. noble ____________________
7. shameful ____________________
8. short, brief ____________________
9. strong ____________________
10. sweet, pleasant ____________________

B. Decline.

Case	M/F		Neuter	
	S.	Pl.	S.	Pl.
nom.	brevis			
gen.				
dat.				
acc.				
abl.				

C. Translate.

1. Art is long and life is short. ____________________
2. matris amici____________________
3. puellarum libri ____________________
4. Romae colles ____________________
5. agricolarum agri ____________________
6. patrum spes____________________
7. Pater puero panem dat.____________________
8. The boys gave father a dog. ____________________

D. Fill in the Blanks.

1. 3rd declension adjectives are related to ____________________ nouns.
2. An ____________________ eats meat and plants.
3. Toad failed to see the ____________________ and ____________________ of his actions and the ____________________ he caused his friends.

 Name____________________ Date ____________

A. Vocabulary: Give dictionary form.

1. beautiful ____________________
2. book ____________________
3. boy ____________________
4. bridge ____________________
5. children ____________________
6. citizen ____________________
7. city ____________________
8. difficult ____________________
9. each, every, all ____________________
10. easy ____________________
11. enemy ____________________
12. evening ____________________
13. faithful ____________________
14. field ____________________
15. free ____________________
16. heavy, serious ____________________
17. hill ____________________
18. knife ____________________
19. lazy ____________________
20. left ____________________
21. man ____________________
22. mountain ____________________
23. noble ____________________
24. part, region ____________________
25. right ____________________
26. sacred ____________________
27. sea ____________________
28. shameful ____________________
29. sharp ____________________
30. ship ____________________
31. short, brief ____________________
32. sick ____________________
33. strong ____________________
34. sweet, pleasant ____________________
35. teacher (male) ____________________
36. teacher (female) ____________________
37. tribe ____________________
38. whole ____________________
39. wretched ____________________

B. Latin Sayings:

1. The Vatican Field ____
2. Our Sea ____
3. Ad astra per áspera. ____
4. Ars longa vita brevis. ____

C. Decline.

S.	Pl.	S.	Pl.	S.	Pl.
puer		pars		mare	

D. Decline the adjectives *liber* and *aeger* in the masculine only.

S.	Pl.
liber	

S.	Pl.
aeger	

Case	M/F		Neuter	
	S.	Pl.	S.	Pl.
nom.	brevis			
gen.				
dat.				
acc.				
abl.				

E. Translate.

1. Rex nautis navem fortem dedit. ______________________________
2. The king's soldiers see the city. ______________________________
3. the sailors' ships ______________________________
4. beautiful sea ______________________________

F. Fill in the Blanks.

1. An indirect object is commonly found with verbs of ______________ or __________.
2. Most 2nd declension nouns and adjectives end in ____________ in the nominative singular, but some end in ____________, and one noun ends in ______________.
3. Third declension nouns that have an **i** in the genitive plural are called ______________.

Lesson 7 Quiz Name_____________________ Date _____________

A. Vocabulary: Give dictionary form.

1. water ______________________
2. moon ______________________
3. fault, blame ______________________
4. anger ______________________
5. forest ______________________
6. star ______________________
7. shadow ______________________
8. wave ______________________
9. bear ______________________
10. life ______________________

B. Decline 1st Person Pronouns with meanings.

Case	Singular	Meaning	Plural	Meaning
nom.				
gen.				
dat.				
acc.				
abl.				

C. Translate.

1. I am the way, the truth, and the life. ____.
2. Ego lunam spectabam. ____
3. Mihi equum dat. ____
4. Nobis aquam dant. ____

D. Fill in the Blanks.

1. The noun the pronoun replaces is called the ____________________________________
2. The genitive of 1st person pronouns is not used to show _________________________.

   It is used for other ________________ expressions.
3. Pronoun Agreement Rule: A pronoun agrees with its ____________________________

   in gender and number, but its ___________is determined by its own clause.
4. Sherwood Forest is a ____________________________________setting.
5. She gave a ______________________performance in the Robin Hood Play.
6. King John was___________________every time Robin Hood escaped.

Lesson 8 Quiz Name____________________ Date ____________

A. Vocabulary: Give dictionary form.

1. money ______________________
2. daughter ______________________
3. Gaul ______________________
4. Spain ______________________
5. Lucy ______________________
6. fatherland ______________________
7. province ______________________
8. victory ______________________
9. grace ______________________
10. road, way ______________________

B. Decline Second Person Pronouns with meanings.

Case	Singular	Meaning	Plural	Meaning
nom.				
gen.				
dat.				
acc.				
abl.				

C. Translate.

1. You too, Brutus? ____
2. Tu Luciam amas. ____
3. Vos amici eritis. ____
4. Vobis provínciam Gálliae damus. ________________________________
5. shameful sins ____
6. I will give you all the lambs.__________________________________

D. Fill in the Blanks.

1. The noun the pronoun replaces is called the ____________________________.
2. The genitive of 2nd person pronouns is not used to show ________________________.
   It is used for other ______ expressions.
3. Pronoun Agreement Rule: A pronoun agrees with its ________________________
   in gender and number, but its ____________ is determined by its own clause.
4. Obedience is a ____________________________ duty.
5. Caesar was __________________________over the Gauls.

Lesson 9 Quiz Name____________________ Date ____________

A. Vocabulary: Give dictionary form.

1. story, tale ____________________
2. woman ____________________
3. eagle ____________________
4. fortune ____________________
5. dawn ____________________
6. island ____________________
7. crown ____________________
8. door ____________________
9. window ____________________
10. kitchen ____________________

B. Decline *noster -tra -trum.*

Case	Singular		
	Masculine	Feminine	Neuter
nominative			
genitive			
dative			
accusative			
ablative			

Case	Plural		
	Masculine	Feminine	Neuter
nominative			
genitive			
dative			
accusative			
ablative			

C. Translate.

1. my fault ____
2. Óppida vestra sunt líbera.________________________________
3. Gállia est pátria tua.__________________________________
4. Templa nostra sunt pulchra. ______________________________
5. Exspectavit fílias meas. ________________________________
6. He plows your field. __________________________________
7. She attended ________________________ school to become a chef.

Lesson 10 Quiz Name____________________ Date ____________

A. Vocabulary: Give dictionary form.

1. gate ________________________
2. seat ________________________
3. altar ________________________
4. letter ________________________
5. farmhouse ________________________

B. Give the Latin for these English prepositions.

Latin	English	Latin	English
	with		in the presence of
	by, from		as far as
	about, down from		under, at the foot of
	in, on		for, on behalf of, in front of
	at the head of		out of, out from
			without

C. Translate.

1. From the founding of the city________________________
2. about Gaul________________________
3. out of the kitchen ________________________
4. with me ________________________
5. without money ________________________
6. He fought for your country. ________________________
7. The Lord be with you (all) ________________________

D. Fill in the Blanks.

1. Prepositions show the ______________________between a noun and another word in the sentence.
2. Prepositions in English that are two or more words are called ______________________ ____.
3. A position with a salary but no responsibility is a ______________________.
4. ______________________________means *to tell before.*

Name______________________ Date ____________

A. Vocabulary: Give dictionary form.

1. plant ______________________
2. cow ______________________
3. writing tablet______________________
4. dinner ______________________
5. crowd ______________________

B. Give the Latin for these English prepositions.

Latin	English	Latin	English
	across		because of
	through		near
	before		between
	against		after, behind
	to, toward, at		among
	around		on account of
	to the foot of		into, onto, against

C. Translate.

1. Hannibal at the gates ____
2. across the river ____
3. against the world ____
4. in the field ______________________ into the field ______________________
5. He saw the cows through the window of the house. ______________________

____

6. They will sail into the harbor. ____

D. Fill in the Blanks.

1. Prepositions take either the ____________________or the __________________cases.
2. The two prepositions that can take both cases are ______________________________.
3. Prepositions in English that are two or more words are called ____________________.

____

4. The first ____were grown in cows.
5. Rough weather on a plane is usually called ______________________________.

 Name______________________ Date ______________

A. Vocabulary: Give dictionary form.

1. life ______________________
2. door ______________________
3. farmhouse ______________________
4. island ______________________
5. road, way ______________________
6. eagle ______________________
7. cow ______________________
8. Spain ______________________
9. bear ______________________
10. green plant ______________________
11. wave ______________________
12. grace, thanks ______________________
13. shadow ______________________
14. Gaul ______________________
15. crowd ______________________
16. daughter ______________________
17. writing tablet ______________________
18. window ______________________
19. forest ______________________
20. woman ______________________
21. story, tale ______________________
22. star ______________________
23. seat ______________________
24. letter ______________________
25. fortune ______________________
26. fault, blame ______________________
27. province ______________________
28. kitchen ______________________
29. crown ______________________
30. gate ______________________
31. money ______________________
32. dinner ______________________
33. dawn ______________________
34. fatherland ______________________
35. altar ______________________
36. moon ______________________
37. Lucy ______________________
38. water ______________________
39. victory ______________________
40. anger ______________________

B. Latin Sayings:

1. Hannibal at the gates ______________________
2. from the founding of the city ______________________
3. my fault ______________________
4. You too, Brutus? ______________________
5. I am the way, the truth, and the life. ______________________

C. Decline.

Case	Singular	Singular	Plural	Plural
nom.	ego	tu	nos	vos
gen.				
dat.				
acc.				
abl.				

D. Give the Latin for these prepositions and check the correct case.

English	Latin	Abl. or Acc.		English	Latin	Abl. or Acc.	
with				without			
through				near			
before				among			
by, from				out of, out from			
to, toward, at				as far as			
about, down from				under, at the foot of			
in the presence of				because of			
across				between			
in, on				for, on behalf of, in front of			
around				after, behind			
to the foot of				into, onto			
at the head of				against			

E. Fill in the Blanks.

1. A pronoun is a word that ____.
2. The word the pronoun is the substitute for is called the ______________________.
3. What is the Latin word for *we*? ____________________ for *us*? ________________
4. The genitive of 1st and 2nd person pronouns is used for ______ expressions that do **not** show ________________________ .
5. To show possession in the 1st and 2nd person, use the possessive pronoun adjectives:
   ____.
6. Give the Adjective Agreement Rule. ____
   ____
7. Give the Pronoun Agreement Rule. ____
   ____
8. Latin prepositions govern either the ________________ or ________________ cases.

 Name____________________ Date ____________

A. Vocabulary: Write a (1) or (2) next to verbs with regular principal parts. For all verbs, give the meaning.

1. accuso ____________________
2. adoro ____________________
3. ámbulo ____________________
4. amo ____________________
5. appáreo ____________________
6. appello ____________________
7. árdeo ____________________
8. aro ____________________
9. cáveo ____________________
10. celo ____________________
11. clamo ____________________
12. creo ____________________
13. culpo ____________________
14. débeo ____________________
15. delecto ____________________
16. demonstro ____________________
17. do ____________________
18. dóceo ____________________
19. dúbito ____________________
20. erro ____________________
21. exploro ____________________
22. exspecto ____________________
23. gáudeo ____________________
24. hábeo ____________________
25. hábito ____________________
26. júbeo ____________________
27. júdico ____________________
28. juvo ____________________
29. laboro ____________________
30. laudo ____________________
31. lavo ____________________
32. líbero ____________________
33. máneo ____________________
34. móneo ____________________
35. móveo ____________________
36. muto ____________________
37. narro ____________________
38. nato ____________________
39. návigo ____________________
40. nego ____________________
41. núntio ____________________
42. óccupo ____________________
43. oppugno ____________________
44. opto ____________________
45. oro ____________________
46. paro ____________________
47. perturbo ____________________
48. porto ____________________
49. prohíbeo ____________________
50. pugno ____________________
51. puto ____________________
52. respóndeo ____________________
53. rogo ____________________
54. saluto ____________________
55. sédeo ____________________
56. servo ____________________
57. specto ____________________
58. spero ____________________
59. sto ____________________
60. sum ____________________
61. súpero ____________________
62. táceo ____________________
63. tempto ____________________
64. téneo ____________________
65. térreo ____________________
66. volo ____________________

B. Latin Sayings:

1. I am a Roman citizen. ______________________________
2. The Mother was standing ______________________________
3. Then we will fight in the shade. ______________________________
4. Let us recite together. ______________________________
5. Beware the dog. ______________________________
6. I see and am silent ______________________________
7. To teach, to delight, to move ______________________________

C. Translate.

1. apparebit ____________________
2. errant ____________________
3. perturbas ____________________
4. perturbabas ____________________
5. mutabamus ____________________
6. optabunt ____________________
7. I was blaming ____________________
8. they fight ____________________
9. you all report ____________________
10. we will hold ____________________
11. I was addressing ____________________
12. they were standing ____________________

D. Fill in the Blanks.

1. The stem vowel of the 1st conjugation is ______________. The stem vowel of the 2nd conjugation is ______________.
2. All verbs whose infinitive ends in ______________ belong to the 1st conjugation.
3. All verbs whose infinitive ends in ______________ belong to the 2nd conjugation.
4. What are the tenses of the present system? ______________________________
____
5. How do you find the present stem for 1st and 2nd conjugation verbs? ______________
____
6. What English helping verbs translate the imperfect tense? ______________________________
7. In English *I praise* is the ____________________ present, *I am praising* is the ____________________ present, and *I do praise* is the ____________________ present.
8. Four 1st conjugation verbs with irregular principal parts are ______________________________
______________________________.

Lesson 13 Quiz Name______________________ Date ______________

A. Vocabulary: Give dictionary form.

1. to convey ________________________
2. to drag ________________________
3. to build ________________________
4. to join ________________________
5. to lead ________________________
6. to live ________________________
7. to say, tell________________________
8. to rule ________________________
9. to conquer ________________________
10. to fix, fasten______________________

B. Conjugate.

Present		Imperfect		Future	
dico					

C. Translate.

1. In this sign you will conquer.____
2. vivimus ____
3. dicet ____
4. tenet ____
5. vincimus ____
6. vinces ____
7. Viri fortes villam in colle struent. ______________________________

D. Fill in the Blanks.

1. The infinitive of 2nd conjugation verbs ends in ____________________; the infinitive of the 3rd conjugation verbs ends in ________________.
2. The 3rd conjugation does not have a stem with a consistent ________________.
3. In the 3rd conjugation the______________________must serve as the present stem.
4. How can you remember the variable vowels in the 3rd conjugation present system?

   ____
5. Why is the 3rd conjugation an old maid?________________________________
6. If you can't be conquered, you are ________________________________.
7. Toad had a ____________________________on motor ________________________.

Lesson 14 Quiz Name____________________ Date ____________

A. Vocabulary: Give dictionary form.

1. to come ____________________
2. to discover ____________________
3. to feel ____________________
4. to finish ____________________
5. to hear ____________________
6. to fortify ____________________
7. to hinder ____________________
8. to know ____________________
9. to not know ____________________
10. to sleep ____________________

B. Conjugate.

Present		Imperfect		Future	
fínio					

C. Translate.

1. I shall either find a way or make one. ____________________
2. múniam ____________________
3. impédient ____________________
4. sentiemus____________________
5. we were sleeping ____________________
6. Ómnium Itáliae provinciarum nómina néscio. ____________________

____

D. Fill in the Blanks.

1. How can you remember the variable vowels in the 3rd and 4th conjugations' present tense? ____________________ future tense?____________________
2. Why are the 3rd and 4th conjugations old maids? ____________________.
3. The infinitive of the 4th conjugation is ____________________.
4. College students often live in a ____________________.
5. There is a ____________________ supply of oil.
6. An ____________________is when you try out for a play or performance.

Lesson 15 Quiz Name____________________ Date ____________

A. Vocabulary: Give dictionary form.

1. to desire ____________________
2. to flee ____________________
3. to make ____________________
4. to take ____________________
5. to throw ____________________

B. Conjugate.

Present		Imperfect		Future	
fácio					

C. Translate.

1. Time flies ____________________
2. fugient ____________________
3. movent ____________________
4. jaciunt ____________________
5. He captures the city. ____________________
6. Mílites fortes trans urbis flumen pontem fácient ____________________

____

D. Fill in the Blanks.

1. The 3rd conjugation does not have a stem with a consistent ____________________.
2. How can you remember the variable vowels in the 3rd, 3rd io, and 4th conjugation present tense? ____________________ future tense? ____________________
3. Why are the 3rd, 3rd io, and 4th conjugations old maids? ____________________

____

4. 3rd **io** verbs belong to the 3rd conjugation because their infinitive ends in __________.
5. 3rd **io** verbs in the present system look exactly like ____________________.
6. ____________________ was the mischievous son of Venus who shot arrows that made people fall in love.
7. A ____________________ is a person who flees from the law.

 Name____________________ Date ____________

A. Vocabulary: Give dictionary form.

1. certain ____________________
2. certainly ____________________
3. happy ____________________
4. happily ____________________
5. long ____________________
6. far, by far ____________________
7. slow ____________________
8. slowly ____________________

B. Give the stem and adverb form for these adjectives:

Adjective	Stem	Adverb
altus -a -um		
latus -a -um		
liber líbera líberum		
asper áspera ásperum		
miser mísera míserum		
pulcher pulchra pulchrum		

Adjective	Stem	Adverb
gravis -e		
fortis -e		
brevis -e		
fidelis -e		
diffícilis -e		
turpis -e		

Adjective	Stem	Adverb
multus -a -um		
facilis		

C. Translate.

1. Make haste slowly ____________________
2. Domum fácile struam. ____________________
3. Fábulas laetē dícimus. ____________________
4. I will speak freely. ____________________

D. Fill in the Blanks.

1. An adverb modifies a ____________________.
2. An adverb most commonly answers the questions ____________________

____________________.

 Name____________________ Date ____________

A. Vocabulary: Give dictionary form.

1. to desire ____________________
2. to flee ____________________
3. to make ____________________
4. to take ____________________
5. to throw ____________________
6. to convey ____________________
7. to drag ____________________
8. to build ____________________
9. to join ____________________
10. to lead ____________________
11. to live ____________________
12. to say, tell____________________
13. to rule ____________________
14. to come ____________________
15. to discover ____________________
16. to feel ____________________
17. to finish ____________________
18. to hear ____________________
19. to fortify ____________________
20. to hinder ____________________
21. to know ____________________
22. to not know ____________________
23. to sleep ____________________
24. to conquer ____________________
25. to fix, fasten____________________
26. happy ____________________
27. happily ____________________
28. slow ____________________
29. slowly ____________________
30. long ____________________
31. far, by far ____________________
32. certain ____________________
33. certainly ____________________
34. beautifully ____________________
35. freely ____________________
36. unhappily ____________________
37. shamefully____________________
38. bravely ____________________

B. Latin Sayings:

1. Time flies ____
2. Make haste slowly ____
3. I shall either find a way or make one. ____
4. In this sign you will conquer. ____

C. Fill in the Blanks.

1. In the 3rd conjugation the ____________________ must serve as the present stem.

2. How can you remember the variable vowels in the 3rd, 3rd **io**, and 4th conjugations' present tense? ____________________ future tense? ____________________

3. Why are the 3rd, 3rd **io,** and 4th conjugations old maids? ____________________

4. All verbs whose infinitive ends in ____________________ belong to the 3rd conjugation.

5. All vcrbs whosc infinitive ends in ______________________ belong to the 4th conjugation.

6. An adverb most commonly modifies a verb by answering the questions ______________________ ____.

7. Most 1st/2nd declension adjectives form adverbs by adding ______________________ to the stem.

8. Most 3rd declension adjectives form adverbs by adding ______________________ to the stem.

9. Some adjectives use the ______________________ singular accusative form as an adverb.

10. 3rd **io** verbs in the present system look exactly like ______________________.

D. Conjugate.

Present	
dico	
Imperfect	
Future	

Present	
vénio	
Imperfect	
Future	

E. Translate.

1. dormis ______________________
2. facit ______________________
3. jáciunt ______________________
4. cápient ______________________
5. áudiam ______________________
6. scimus ______________________
7. I will come ______________________
8. they conquer ______________________
9. you all were living ______________________
10. they will say ______________________
11. we flee ______________________
12. he was leading ______________________

 Name____________________ Date ____________

A. Vocabulary: Give first two principal parts for 1-30 and all principal parts for 31-40.

1. to wound ______________________
2. to fly ______________________
3. to call ______________________
4. to desire, wish______________________
5. to tell ______________________
6. to judge ______________________
7. to live in ______________________
8. to doubt ______________________
9. to show ______________________
10. to blame ______________________
11. to report ______________________
12. to fight ______________________
13. to disturb ______________________
14. to hide ______________________
15. to accuse ______________________
16. to walk ______________________
17. to change ______________________
18. to attack ______________________
19. to frighten ______________________
20. to tempt ______________________
21. to appear ______________________
22. to love ______________________
23. to have ______________________
24. to work ______________________
25. to plow ______________________
26. to seize ______________________
27. to speak, pray ______________________
28. to think ______________________
29. to wait for ______________________
30. to err ______________________
31. to see ____
32. to move ____
33. to be strong____
34. to respond ____
35. to teach ____
36. to burn____
37. to order ____
38. to help ____
39. to hold____
40. to give ____

B. Conjugate.

Perfect		Pluperfect		Future Perfect	
fui					

Perfect		Pluperfect		Future Perfect	
amavi					

C. Translate.

1. clamávimus ______________________
2. mansit ______________________
3. vídimus ______________________
4. arsisti ______________________
5. lavistis ______________________
6. they will have stood ______________
7. they stayed ______________________
8. he had seen ______________________
9. I hoped ______________________
10. hsi has been silent ______________

D. Latin Sayings:

1. I came, I saw, I conquered. ____
2. Pray and work. ____
3. To err is human. ____
4. Now or never ____
5. Fortune aids the brave. ____
6. Always faithful ____

E. Fill in the Blanks.

1. How many Latin conjugations are there?___. Name them. ______________________
2. How do you find the present stem for 1st, 2nd, and 4th conjugation verbs? __________
   ____
3. What are the tenses of the perfect system?______________________________________
   ____
4. How do you find the perfect stem for all conjugations? ____________________________
   ____
5. What English helping verb translates the pluperfect tense? ______________________
   What English helping verbs translate the future perfect tense? __________________

Lesson 18 Quiz Name____________________ Date ____________

A. Give the four principal parts for each verb.

1. to rule ______________________________
2. to say, speak, tell ______________________________
3. to lead ______________________________
4. to fix, fasten ______________________________
5. to join ______________________________
6. to build, construct ______________________________
7. to drag, haul ______________________________
8. to carry, convey, transport ______________________________
9. to live ______________________________
10. to conquer ______________________________

B. Conjugate.

Perfect		Pluperfect		Future Perfect	
dixi					

C. Translate.

1. The master has spoken. ______________

____

2. vicit ______________________________
3. traxistis ______________________________
4. dúxerat ______________________________
5. véxerit ______________________________
6. vixéritis ______________________________
7. I will have ruled ______________________________
8. they had fixed ______________________________
9. she had joined ______________________________
10. you dragged ______________________________
11. they said ______________________________

D. Fill in the Blanks.

1. What vowels appear in the present tense of the 3rd conjugation? ______________
2. What vowels appear in the future tense of the 3rd conjugation? ______________
3. Why is the 3rd conjugation imperfect tense easy to remember? ______________
4. All verbs whose infinitive ends in ________belong to the 3rd conjugation.
5. How do you find the perfect stem for all four conjugations? ______________

____

6. What is the pattern for principal parts for all but two of the verbs in this lesson? ______

____

 Name____________________ Date ____________

A. Give all four principal parts.

1. to hear ______________________________
2. to sleep______________________________
3. to finish, limit______________________________
4. to fortify______________________________
5. to know ______________________________
6. to not know ______________________________
7. to hinder, impede______________________________
8. to come______________________________
9. to discover, find out______________________________
10. to feel ______________________________

B. Conjugate.

Perfect		Pluperfect		Future Perfect	
veni					

C. Translate.

1. From sea to sea ____________________

____

2. audíverat ____________________
3. dormívimus ____________________
4. finivisti ____________________
5. invenisti ____________________
6. nescíveris ____________________
7. I heard ____________________
8. they finished ____________________
9. they will have known ____________________
10. she fortified ____________________
11. I hindered ____________________

D. Fill in the Blanks.

1. The present system of the 4th conjugation is essentially the same as the present system of the 3rd conjugation with the addition of ______________________________.
2. All verbs whose infinitive ends in ________ belong to the 4th conjugation.
3. The perfect system of all four conjugations is ____________________regular.
4. How do you find the perfect stem for all four conjugations? ____________________

____

Lesson 20 Quiz Name____________________ Date ____________

A. Give all four principal parts.

1. to take, capture ____
2. to desire ____
3. to make, do ____
4. to throw, hurl ____
5. to flee ____

B. Conjugate.

Perfect		Pluperfect		Future Perfect	
feci					

C. Translate.

1. Said and done ____________________
2. fugeramus ____________________
3. céperas ____________________
4. fécerint ____________________
5. cupivi ____________________
6. jeci ____________________
7. he took ____________________
8. she had desired____________________
9. we made ____________________
10. they fled ____________________
11. you had taken ____________________
12. you all threw ____________________

D. Fill in the Blanks.

1. What vowels appear in the present tense of the 3rd and 4th conjugation? ____________
2. The present system of the 4th conjugation is essentially the same as the 3rd conjugation with the addition of ____.
3. All verbs whose infinitive ends in ________belong to the 3rd conjugation.
4. 3rd **io** verbs belong to the 3rd conjugation because their infinitive ends in ____________.
5. 3rd **io** verbs in the present system look exactly like ____________________.
6. What three 3rd io verbs form their perfect stem with a vowel change? ______________

____

Lesson 21 Quiz Name____________________ Date ____________

A. Vocabulary.

1. quis ______________________
2. quomodo ______________________
3. quid ______________________
4. quando ______________________
5. quam diu ______________________
6. ubi ______________________
7. quot ______________________
8. cur ______________________

B. Translate.

1. Quid novi?______________________
2. Dicebatne? ______________________
3. Vincebantne? ______________________
4. Audiuntne? ______________________
5. Vēnitne? ______________________
6. Cepitne? ______________________
7. Will he say/tell? ______________________
8. Will they conquer? ______________________
9. Do you hear? ______________________
10. Do they come? ______________________
11. Did they take?______________________
12. Nihil! ______________________

C. Translate.

1. Dabitne rex poetae pigro donum?______________________

____

2. Quid fecisti? ______________________
3. Quomodo vales?______________________
4. Quot domūs struxisti?______________________
5. Cur tu malus sentis? ______________________

D. Fill in the Blanks.

1. How do you find the perfect stem for all four conjugations? ______________________

____

2. What are the two types of direct questions? ______________________

____

3. How do you form yes or no questions in English?______________________

____

4. How do you form yes or no questions in Latin?______________________

____

5. Give the six common questions words in English.______________________

____

 Name_____________________ Date ______________

A. Give all four principal parts for verbs.

English	Latin
to build, construct	
to come	
to conquer	
to convey, transport	
to desire	
to discover, find out	
to drag, haul	
to feel	
to finish	
to fix, fasten	
to flee	
to fortify, protect	
to hear	
to hinder, obstruct	
to join, connect	
to know	
to know not	
to lead	
to live, be alive	
to make, do	
to rule	
to say, speak, tell	
to sleep	
to take, capture	
to throw, hurl	
who?	
what?	
when?	
where?	
why?	
how many?	
how long?	
how (in what manner)?	

 Name____________________ Date ____________

B. Conjugate *scio, capio,* and *rego* in the Perfect System.

Perfect		Pluperfect		Future Perfect	

Perfect		Pluperfect		Future Perfect	

Perfect		Pluperfect		Future Perfect	

C. Latin Sayings:

1. The master has spoken. ____________________
2. From sea to sea ____________________
3. Said and done ____________________
4. What's new? ____________________

D. Translate.

1. fugerunt ____________________
2. audivit ____________________
3. dúxerat ____________________
4. jeci ____________________
5. fixit ____________________
6. they made ____________________
7. I had known ____________________
8. we built ____________________
9. hsi lived ____________________
10. you came ____________________

E. Translate.

1. Quam diu victoriam impedies? ____________________
2. Quando pontem munies? ____________________
3. Fugiesne nobiscum cras? ____________________
4. Habetne tuus frater multam pecuniam? ____________________

____

5. Quot vaccas habet. ____________________

____

 Name____________________ Date ____________

A. Vocabulary: Give dictionary form.

1. wolf ______________________
2. food ______________________
3. a Gaul ______________________
4. Mark ______________________
5. field, plain ______________________
6. garden ______________________
7. wind ______________________
8. game, school ______________________
9. place ______________________
10. cloud, storm cloud ______________________

B. Conjugate *laudo* in the present tense, passive voice, with singular meanings.

Present Passive		Meaning - Present Passive Singular
laudor		

C. Translate.

1. laudantur ______________________
2. rogatur ______________________
3. amamur ______________________
4. vocaris ______________________
5. judicámini ______________________

D. Translate.

1. A friend is proven in time of necessity. ______________________
1. Hortus ab agrícolis aratur. ______________________
2. Puer a magistris laudatur. ______________________

E. Fill in the Blanks.

1. In the ______________________ voice, the subject performs the action of the verb.
   In the ______________________ voice, the subject receives the action of the verb.
2. When the action of the passive verb is performed by a LIVING THING, the construction is called ______________________
   and requires the preposition ______________________ .
3. Give the active and passive personal endings.

Active		Passive	

Lesson 23 Quiz Name____________________ Date ____________

A. Vocabulary: Give dictionary form.

1. lieutenant______________________
2. ally ______________________
3. mind, spirit ______________________
4. eye ______________________
5. barbarian, foreigner ______________
6. a Christian ______________________
7. a Roman ______________________
8. student ______________________
9. people ______________________
10. sword ______________________

B. Conjugate *laudo* in the imperfect and future passive.

Imperfect Passive	

Future Passive	

C. Translate.

1. laudabuntur______________________
2. rogabatur ______________________
3. amabamur ______________________
4. vocáberis ______________________
5. judicabímini ______________________

D. Translate.

1. He is known by his companions ______________________
2. Christiani a Romanis non amabantur. ______________________

____

3. Tu a populo laudaberis ______________________

E. Fill in the Blanks.

1. In the ______________________voice, the subject performs the action of the verb.
   In the ______________________voice, the subject receives the action of the verb.
2. When the action of the passive verb is performed by a LIVING THING, the construction is called ______________________
   and requires the preposition ______________________ .
3. Give the active and passive personal endings.

Active		Passive	

Lesson 24 Quiz Name____________________ Date ____________

A. Vocabulary: Give dictionary form.

1. shield ____________________
2. wine ____________________
3. neck ____________________
4. back, rear ____________________
5. silver ____________________
6. gold ____________________
7. wood ____________________
8. iron, tool ____________________
9. wall, rampart____________________
10. missile ____________________

B. Conjugate *video* in the present system active and passive.

Present Active		Imperfect Active		Future Active	

Present Passive		Imperfect Passive		Future Passive	

C. Translate.

1. móneor ____________________
2. videbitur ____________________
3. docebamini ____________________
4. moneberis ____________________
5. tenemur ____________________
6. Iron is sharpened by iron. ____________________
7. Vir auro temptatur. ____________________
8. Mílites telis terrebantur. ____________________

D. Fill in the blanks.

1. When the action of the passive verb is performed by a NON-LIVING THING, the construction is called ____________________, and the preposition is ____________________.
2. Give the one irregularity in the present system passive of the 1st and 2nd conjugations. ____________________
3. This country's name means silver. ____________________

 Name____________________ Date ____________

A. Vocabulary: Give dictionary form.

1. joy ______________________
2. sign ______________________
3. reward ______________________
4. leaf ______________________
5. battle ______________________
6. grain, corn ______________________
7. sin, mistake ______________________
8. age, time, period______________________
9. arm, forearm ______________________
10. zeal, enthusiasm, study __________

B. Conjugate *duco* in the present system active and passive.

Present Active		Imperfect Active		Future Active	

Present Passive		Imperfect Passive		Future Passive	

C. Translate.

1. ducuntur ____
2. figebatur____
3. figor ____
4. dícimur ____
5. regetur ____
6. Repetition is the mother of learning.______________________________
7. Canis manu figebatur. ______________________________
8. Cives lege reguntur. ______________________________

D. Fill in the Blanks.

1. What is the one irregularity in the present system passive of the 3rd conjugation?
   ____
2. What is the one irregularity in the present system passive of the first two conjugations?
   ____
3. This English word for small mistake or sin,______________________________, comes from a similar Spanish word.

 Name____________________ Date ____________

A. Vocabulary: Give dictionary form.

1. shout, cry ______________________
2. senator ______________________
3. grief, pain ______________________
4. tree ______________________
5. work, toil ______________________
6. general, commander ____________
7. shepherd, pastor ______________
8. speaker, orator ______________
9. fisherman ______________________
10. love, passion ________________

B. Translate.

1. The city which captured the whole world is now captured. ______________________

____

2. Spíritus meus dolore superatur. ______________________________________
3. Oratorum clamores a cívibus audientur. ________________________________

____

4. Filius tuus amore vincetur. ____

C. Fill in the Blanks.

1. What is the one irregularity in the present system passive of the 3rd and 3rd **io** conjugations? ____
2. What is the one irregularity in the present system passive of the first two conjugations?

   ____

3. When the action of the passive verb is performed by a LIVING THING, the construction is called ____
   and requires the preposition ____.
4. When the action of a verb is performed by a NON-LIVING THING, the construction is called ____,
   and the preposition is ____.

 Name____________________ Date ____________

D. Conjugations.

Conjugate **áudio** in the present system active and passive.

Present Active	

Present Passive	

Imperfect Active	

Imperfect Passive	

Future Active	

Future Passive	

Conjugate **cápio** in the present system active and passive.

Present Active	

Present Passive	

Imperfect Active	

Imperfect Passive	

Future Active	

Future Passive	

Name_____________________ Date _____________

A. Vocabulary: Give dictionary form.

English	Latin
1. grain, corn	
2. sin, mistake	
3. wine	
4. mind, spirit	
5. joy	
6. people	
7. neck	
8. Mark	
9. missile	
10. grief, pain	
11. eye	
12. wall, rampart	
13. tree	
14. sword	
15. reward	
16. food	
17. school, game	
18. ally	
19. barbarian, foreigner	
20. work	
21. age, time period	
22. shout, cry	
23. a Gaul	
24. wolf	
25. leaf	

English	Latin
26. shepherd	
27. fisherman	
28. zeal, study, enthusiasm	
29. a Christian	
30. place, location	
31. sign	
32. silver	
33. garden	
34. battle	
35. iron, iron tool	
36. orator	
37. wind	
38. student	
39. cloud, storm cloud	
40. back	
41. forearm	
42. lieutenant	
43. shield	
44. gold	
45. general, commander	
46. a Roman	
47. field, plain	
48. wood	
49. senator	
50. love	

B. Conjugate each verb in the present system passive.

laudo (1st)

Present Passive	

Imperfect Passive	

Future Passive	

rego (3rd)

Present Passive	

Imperfect Passive	

Future Passive	

cápio (3rd **io**)

Present Passive	

Imperfect Passive	

Future Passive	

áudio (4th)

Present Passive	

Imperfect Passive	

Future Passive	

C. Latin Sayings:

1. Iron is sharpened by iron ______________________
2. He is known by his companions ______________________
3. A friend is proven in a time of necessity. ______________________
4. Repetition is the mother of learning. ______________________
5. The city which captured the whole world is captured. ______________________

____

D. Form Drills:

1. audiuntur ______________________
2. figebatur ______________________
3. móneor ______________________
4. regebamur ______________________
5. laudabímini ______________________

E. Translate. Underline the ablative of agent or ablative of means.

1. Cives vento terrebantur. ______________________
2. Lupus a pastóribus oppugnabitur. ______________________
3. Discípuli a magistro laudantur. ______________________
4. Vir cultro vulneratur. ______________________
5. Exércitus ab imperatóribus dúcitur. ______________________
6. The money will be taken by the disgraceful citizens. ______________________

   ____
7. The work was finished by the students. ______________________

   ____
8. The grain was taken by the lazy shepherds. ______________________

   ____

Second Form
Final Examination

A. Grammar

1. Some nouns have only plural forms. An example is ______________________.

2. Four confusing words with the root of **liber** are ______________________
____

3. Name the four verb complements you have learned. ______________________
____

4. What are the two types of adjectives in Latin? ______________________

5. Third declension adjectives are related to ______________________.

6. How many kinds of pronouns are there? Name them in pairs. ______________________
____
____

7. The perfect system is ______________________ regular in all four conjugations.

8. How do you find the perfect stem for all four conjugations? ______________________
____

9. Although 3rd conjugation verbs do not have regular principal parts, they do have ______
______________________ that will help you remember them.

10. What is the pattern for verbs like **rego**? ______________________

11. What are the two types of direct questions? ______________________
____

12. How do you form yes or no questions in English? ______________________

13. How do you form yes or no questions in Latin? ______________________
____

14. Give the six common question words in English. ______________________
____

15. Give the two voices of Latin verbs. ______________________

B. Vocabulary

Check the correct gender, give genitive form and meaning.

English	M.	F.	N.	Meaning
1. órator				
2. peccatum				
3. mare				
4. culpa				
5. óculus				
6. discípulus				
7. aurum				
8. ludus				
9. collis				
10. culina				
11. via				
12. vesper				
13. villa				
14. turba				
15. telum				
16. amor				
17. frumentum				
18. piscator				
19. vir				
20. jánua				
21. scutum				
22. epístula				
23. urbs				
24. fólium				
25. fenestra				

B. Vocabulary, cont.

Check the part of speech (adjective, adverb, pronoun, or preposition) and give meaning.

English	Adj.	Adv.	Pro.	Prep.	Meaning
1. brevis -e					
2. cum					
3. tu, tui					
4. multum					
5. íntegER -gra -grum					
6. laetus -a -um					
7. túrpiter					
8. fortis -e					
9. bréviter					
10. lentus -a -um					
11. trans					
12. laetē					
13. asper -a -um					
14. fácile					
15. pro					
16. dulcis -e					
17. de					
18. post					
19. piger -gra -grum					
20. apud					
21. ex					
22. ab					
23. aeger -gra -grum					
24. sine					
25. ego, mei					

C. Conjugations, cont.

Conjugate **amo** in the indicative active, present and perfect systems; and in the present system passive with meanings as shown.

present stem__________________

Present Active	

Present Passive	

Imperfect Active	

Imperfect Passive	

Future Active	

Future Passive	

perfect stem__________________________

Present Passive Meanings

Perfect	

Present Passive Meanings, Sing. only

Pluperfect	

Imperfect Passive Meanings, Sing. only

Future Perfect	

Future Passive Meanings, Sing. only

C. Conjugations, cont.

Conjugate **móneo** in the indicative active, present and perfect systems; and in the present system passive with meanings as shown.

present stem__________________

Present Active	

Present Passive	

Imperfect Active	

Imperfect Passive	

Future Active	

Future Passive	

perfect stem__________________________

Perfect	

Pluperfect	

Future Perfect	

Present Passive Meanings

Present Passive Meanings, Sing. only

Imperfect Passive Meanings, Sing. only

Future Passive Meanings, Sing. only

C. Conjugations, cont.

Conjugate **rego** in the indicative active, present and perfect systems; and in the present system passive with meanings as shown.

present stem________________

Present Active	

Present Passive	

Imperfect Active	

Imperfect Passive	

Future Active	

Future Passive	

perfect stem______________________

Present Passive Meanings

Perfect	

Present Passive Meanings, Sing. only

Pluperfect	

Imperfect Passive Meanings, Sing. only

Future Perfect	

Future Passive Meanings, Sing. only

C. Conjugations, cont.

Conjugate **áudio** in the indicative active, present and perfect systems; and in the present system passive with as shown.

present stem__________________

Present Active	

Present Passive	

Imperfect Active	

Imperfect Passive	

Future Active	

Future Passive	

perfect stem__________________________

Perfect	

Pluperfect	

Future Perfect	

Present Passive Meanings

Present Passive Meanings, Sing. only

Imperfect Passive Meanings, Sing. only

Future Passive Meanings, Sing. only

C. Conjugations, cont.

Conjugate **cápio** in the indicative active, present and perfect systems; and in the present system passive with as shown.

present stem__________________

Present Active	

Present Passive	

Imperfect Active	

Imperfect Passive	

Future Active	

Future Passive	

perfect stem__________________________

Present Passive Meanings

Perfect	

Present Passive Meanings, Sing. only

Pluperfect	

Imperfect Passive Meanings, Sing. only

Future Perfect	

Future Passive Meanings, Sing. only

D. Declensions

Singular	Plural
vir	

Singular	Plural
puer	

Singular	Plural
ager	

Singular	Plural
liber (noun)	

Singular	Plural
pars	

Singular	Plural
mare	

M/F

Singular	Plural
brevis	

N

Singular	Plural

D. Declensions, cont.

Singular

Masculine	Feminine	Neuter
integer		

Plural

Masculine	Feminine	Neuter

Singular	Plural
ego	

Singular Meaning	Plural Meaning

Singular	Plural
tu	

Singular Meaning	Plural Meaning

E. Latin Sayings

1. The Vatican Field ______
2. Our Sea ______
3. To the stars through difficulties. ______
4. Art is long and life is short. ______
5. Hannibal at the gates ______
6. from the founding of the city ______
7. my fault ______
8. You too, Brutus? ______
9. I am the way, the truth, and the life. ______
10. In this sign you will conquer. ______
11. I shall either find a way or make one. ______
12. Time flies ______
13. Make haste slowly ______
14. The master has spoken. ______
15. From sea to sea ______
16. Said and done ______
17. What's new? ______
18. Iron is sharpened by iron ______
19. He is known by his companions ______
20. A friend is proven in a time of necessity. ______
21. Repetition is the mother of learning. ______
22. The city which captured the whole world is now captured. ______

______

F. Form Drills

1. finimur ______________________
2. scies ______________________
3. jungebant ______________________
4. invénior ______________________
5. vici ______________________
6. amabor ______________________
7. audiebamini ______________________
8. jácitur ______________________
9. monetur ______________________
10. dixerat ______________________

G. Translation

1. Viri fortes dolorem sciunt. ______________________
2. Tu nos doces. ______________________
3. Púeri pater sorori panem dat. ______________________
4. Scisne viri dolorem? ______________________
5. Scivi fortem virum. ______________________
6. Fortes viros sciverunt. ______________________
7. Pons novus ínsulam vestram ad terras gentis nostrae junxit. ______________________
____
8. Frumentum ex agrícolae agris fácile capiebatur. ______________________
____
9. Patris amici mihi de bello fábulas narrabant. ______________________
____
10. In colle alto scuta et ferra Gallorum facile videntur. ______________________
____
11. I heard the waves of the sea and saw the ships of our country. ______________________
____
12. Gold will be discovered in the mountains of Gaul. ______________________
____